Nefertiti Presents . . .

Belly Dancing

"the Basics"

Nefertiti Presents . . .

Belly Dancing
"the Basics"

Sherry Jeffries
(Ankestamen)

Mud Puddle Books
NEW YORK

Nefertiti Presents…
Belly Dancing
"the Basics"
Written by Sherry Jeffries
            (Ankestamen)

Published by
Mud Puddle Books, Inc.
54 W. 21st Street
Suite 601
New York, NY 10010

info@mudpuddlebooks.com

ISBN: 978-1-60311-024-2

Printed and bound in China

This is dedicated to my mother
Doris Nemeth/Demarest
(AKA, Nefertiti)
for all her hard work
during my childhood.
I Love you Mom!

Contents

Introduction

Welcome to "Belly Dancing, the Basics", I am your host "Nefertiti".

This book is designed to help you learn the basic beginning moves of Middle Eastern Dance. It is best used as a learning aid while taking classes from a professional teacher.

Practice the move 10 to 12 times each. Always practice the moves on both sides of the body (left and right).

And most of all "Have Fun"!

Cymbals (Zills)

◈ Put one zill on your thumb, the other on your middle finger

   ⸙ Do not slide past the first knuckle

◈ Adjust your elastic to fit snug, but not too tight. Cut off excess elastic to prevent interference with the sound

◈ Hit your finger and thumb together, releasing very quickly

   ⸙ You want a "ting" sound not a "thud"

◈ The basic pattern is
   (R) right, (L) left, (R) Right, (_) pause

◈ Repeat

RLR_RLR_RLR_RLR
(Sounding like a horse gallop)

Basic Position

- ❖ We start in a standing position with legs parallel
- ❖ Pretend to walk forward 1 step
- ❖ Keep that foot forward, bend both knees
- ❖ Put all your weight on the back leg
- ❖ Keep your buttocks tucked under your body
- ❖ Arms are out away from your body and held high
- ❖ Chest is held high, not caved in
- ❖ Stomach is tight

Never lock your knees unless otherwise told. Always keep them bent or you may cause damage to your knees.

Changing Legs in Basic Position

- ❖ To change legs in basic position, pick up your front leg, place it back down again, and step forward with your other leg. Just like you were taking a step
- ❖ You are now back in basic position and ready for moves on that leg

Hip-Lift, Hip-Drop
(Bounce)

◈ Start in basic position with right leg forward

◈ Lift your right hip *"Pretend to have a string tied to your hip bone, and somebody is pulling up on it"*

◈ Drop your hip *"Just let it fall back to normal position"*

◈ Lift your hip again and drop it

◈ Continue this at a faster pace until it becomes a bounce

Hip lift

Hip drop

Side View

Half-Moon

❖ In basic position

❖ Lift your hip, pivot your hip around in a half circle (half moon) to the front, and drop it

❖ Lift hip, pivot it around to the back, and drop it

❖ Lift hip, pivot to the front, and drop it

❖ Lift hip, pivot to the back, and drop it.

❖ Repeat until it becomes a continuous, smooth, move

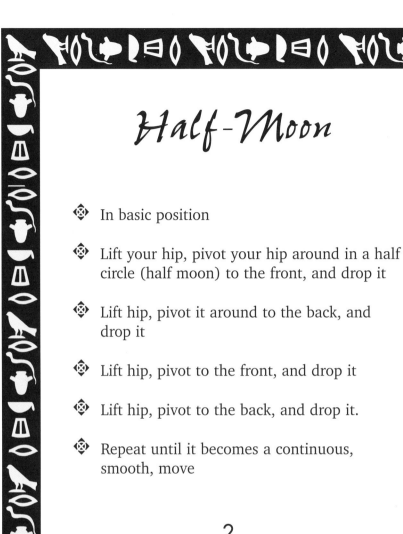

2
Hip lift
1   3

Side View

Parallel Position

❖ Stand with both legs parallel facing front, bend your knees, chest up, arms out, buttocks tucked in

❖ ***This is known as "Parallel Position"***

Hip Thrust

❖ Stand in parallel position

❖ Twist your hips pushing one hip forward

❖ In a washing-machine style, twist your waist so the other hip is forward

❖ Repeat left, right, left, right

❖ This is the "Hip Thrust"

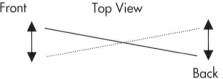

Pretend you have a table in front of you, and you want to knock the table hard with your hip bone. Now twist and hit the table with the other hip.

Hip Shimmy
(Shake)

❖ Continue with the hip thrust, but make the hip thrust smaller and speed it up faster, and faster (*pretend someone put one of the straps from a vibration machine around your buttocks and turned it on*)

❖ When the move is done correctly, your hips are moving so quickly your buttocks is shaking (back and forth, not up and down) This is the "Hip Shake"

Marching with Hip Shimmy

❖ While continuing the hip shake, take your left foot and baby step forward

❖ Now right foot, left, right, until your marching forward

❖ This can be done forward or backward

Sit-Kick Front
(also known as Egyptian Basic)

- ❖ We start this move in parallel position

- ❖ Pretend to "sit" in a chair by bending both knees (squatting position)

- ❖ When you sit, your left foot pivots to the left, your left knee turns out to the left, and your left hip drops

- ❖ To kick, begin returning to standing position, while turning your whole left leg and foot around to the right causing your hip to snap to the front

- ❖ Repeat, "Sit-Kick Front"

Sit-Kick Side

❖ Standing in parallel position

❖ Bend both knees to "sit"

❖ To "kick" begin to stand

❖ Do not turn your leg around, just straighten it and push your hip to the side

❖ Repeat, "Sit-Kick Side"

Pretend there is a table to your side and you wish to hit the table with your hip—also, for those who have done the dance "The Bump", think of bumping to the side.

Back View

Sit-Kick Back

❖ Standing in parallel position, move the leg slightly behind the other leg

❖ To "sit", bend both knees a couple of inches, then straighten the back one pushing your buttock out backward giving a kick to the back

❖ When you bend your leg your buttock should drop back to parallel

❖ Bend straighten, bend straighten

❖ Repeat, "Sit-Kick Back"

Set-Kick, Front, Side, and Back can be done as a 3-way move, doing each one time followed by the next move. Repeat at the end.

Sit-Kick Side

Sit-Kick Side

Lean-Kick

◈ Stand in parallel position

◈ Bend both knees

◈ You are going to sway like a pendulum to the left side, going lower in the middle

◈ Once you reach the side, straighten your leg with a sit-kick side

◈ Now, sway to the other side, and straighten that leg with a sit-kick side

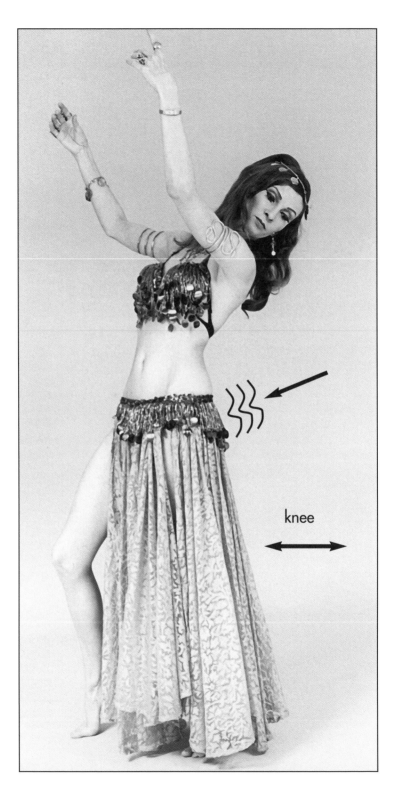

knee

Single Leg Shimmy

- ❖ Stand in basic position

- ❖ With your weight on the back foot, slightly bend your back knee

- ❖ Straighten it back

- ❖ Bend, straighten. Repeat very quickly

- ❖ This becomes a small vibration of the leg causing the lower buttock to shimmy

- ❖ While doing this move, look over your shoulder to emphasize the area of movement

knees

Two Leg Shimmy

❖ Stand in parallel position

❖ With your weight on both feet, slightly bend your left knee

❖ Straighten it back

❖ Slightly bend your right knee

❖ Straighten it back

❖ Alternate knees in very small movements

❖ Repeat very quickly

❖ This becomes a small vibration of the legs causing the lower buttocks and upper legs to "shimmy"

This move can be reversed to go forward

Also this move can be done upwards (sway) and downwards (Maya)

Figure 8
Backward

❖ Start in parallel position. Bend your knees

❖ Start by pushing one hip out to the front

❖ Slowly and smoothly move your hip in a half circle around toward the back

❖ When you get to the back, bring your other hip to the front

❖ Slowly and smoothly move your other hip in a half circle around to the back

❖ When you get to the back, bring your other hip to the front

❖ Repeat this until it becomes a continuous smooth "Figure 8"

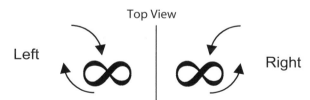

Top View

Left   Right

This move is done with the shoulders, the bust or bust size has nothing to do with it. Your costume should be made with a well-fitting, supportive bra to give you added protection.

Shoulder Thrust and Shoulder (Bust) Shimmy

- ❖ Begin in basic position

- ❖ Hold your chest up

- ❖ Push the right shoulder to the front, and the left shoulder to the back

- ❖ Switch position, push the right shoulder to the back, and the left shoulder to the front

- ❖ This thrusting movement is the "Shoulder Thrust"

Shoulder (Bust) Shimmy

- ❖ Make the move very small and very quick until your shoulders shimmy: "think of the 1960's"

- ❖ This is the shoulder shake

Shoulder Roll

- ❖ Start by standing In basic position

- ❖ Take one shoulder and roll in backward

- ❖ Take the other shoulder and roll it backward

- ❖ Alternate each shoulder in a rolling backward motion

- ❖ With each roll back, lower your self by bending your knees and leaning backward

- ❖ Do a bust shake while rising your self back up to standing position

Keep the moves small.

*This move can be done
with many variations
of beats, and speed.
Try different variations
according to
your music.*

Pelvic Tilt

❖ Stand in parallel position

❖ Tilt your pelvis up by tucking your buttocks in

❖ Untuck by tilting your pelvis back, causing your buttocks to stick out

❖ Tilt, untilt

❖ This move should be done with small tilts. *Over use and over exaggerating this move will make it look vulgar*

❖ For each tilt bend your knees a little, do three consecutive tilts while lowering and then return to standing position

❖ Tilt, tilt, tilt, up, repeat

Side Profile

Drop rib-cage
and stick
stomach out

Stomach in

Rib-cage up

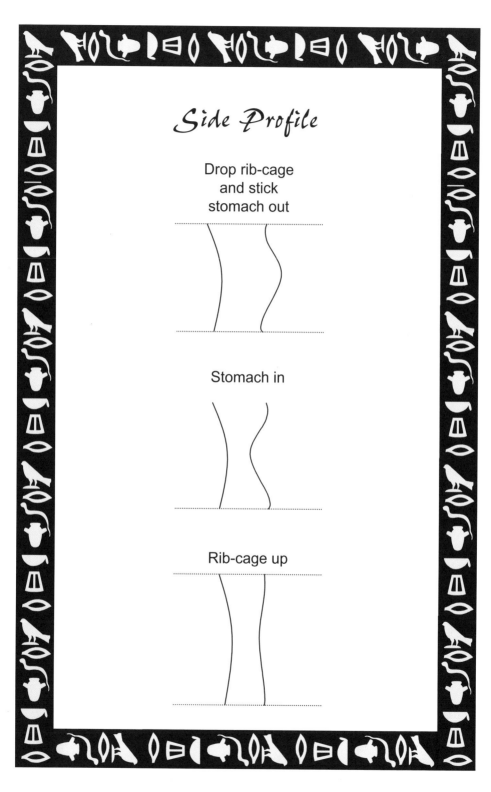

Belly Roll

◈ Standing in basic position

◈ Drop your rib-cage (like exhaling) and stick your stomach out as far as you can

◈ Suck it in as far as you can

◈ Pull up with your rib-cage

◈ Drop, stick out your stomach, suck it in, pull up (out, in, up)

◈ This move takes a lot of practice to make it a smooth continuous movement

◈ PRACTICE, PRACTICE, PRACTICE

Head Movements

This movement is all done with the neck

- ❖ Put your arms above your head in a triangle

- ❖ With your neck, try to touch your left ear to your (inside) left elbow (do not bend your head to your shoulder)

- ❖ Pull your neck back to move head backward

- ❖ Touch your right ear to the (inside) right elbow

- ❖ Push your neck to the front to move the head forward

Right, left, right, left, and around
(Usually done to slow music)

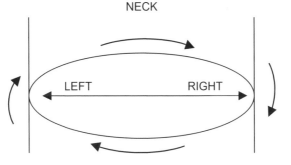

NECK

LEFT   RIGHT

47

Snake Arms

This move can be done in big snake arms or little snake arms. The main thing is to round your elbows, and make the move smooth.

Snake Arms

❖ Start with both arms down by your sides.

❖ Round your arms.

❖ Lift your left shoulder. Slowly raise your left elbow. Begin raising your left wrist. Continue raising your left wrist above your elbow. Bend your left forearm above your head and slowly flip your wrist backward so the back of your hand is above your head

❖ Lift your right shoulder and lower your left shoulder. Slowly raise your right elbow while lowering your left elbow (you should look like a sideways "S". Begin raising your right wrist while lowering your left wrist. Continue raising your right wrist above your elbow while lowering your left wrist below your elbow. Bend your right arm above your head and bend your left arm below your elbow. Slowly flip your right wrist backward so the back of your hand is above your head and your left wrist under

❖ Continue switching arms, with each arm doing exactly the opposite of the other

Veil Work

Most of the time done to
slow (or slower) music
Can be done fast for Gypsy style

While transitioning from one veil move
to another, never stop moving.
Do shimmies, belly rolls,
figure 8's etc.

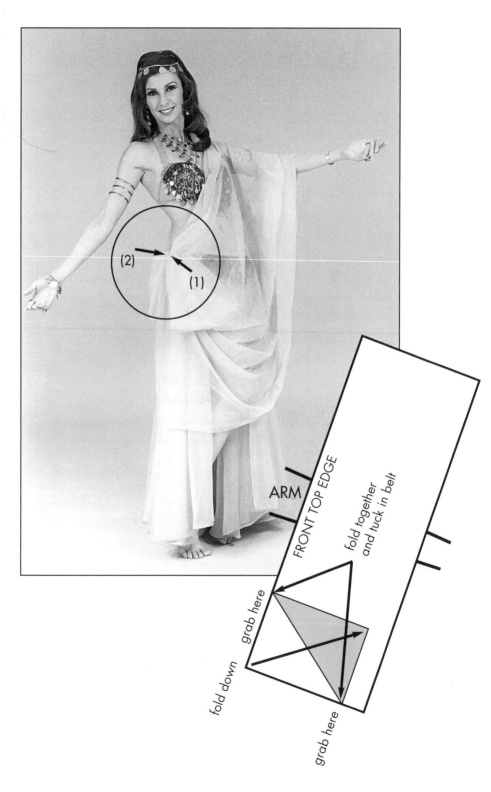

(2)

(1)

FRONT TOP EDGE

ARM

fold together
and tuck in belt

grab here

fold down

grab here

Veil

*2½ to 3 yards (2.3 to 2.75 m) of
a lightweight chiffon, silk, or other
material which moves freely*

Drape (Wrap) (traditional style)

❖ Hold your arm out and drape the veil over
your arm even on both sides *(If you are
right handed drape it over your left arm)*

❖ Slide your hand down the front top edge of
the veil, till about 6 inches (15 cm) from the
corner stop and hold it

❖ Now hold the side edge 6 inches (15 cm)
below the top corner edge

❖ Put the two edges together to make a fold,
which will leave a pocket hanging

❖ Tuck the fold into the side of your belt
opposite the arm holding the veil (1)

❖ Reach behind you and grab the other side
of the half of the veil

❖ Do the same fold with the corners and tuck
right behind the first tuck (2)

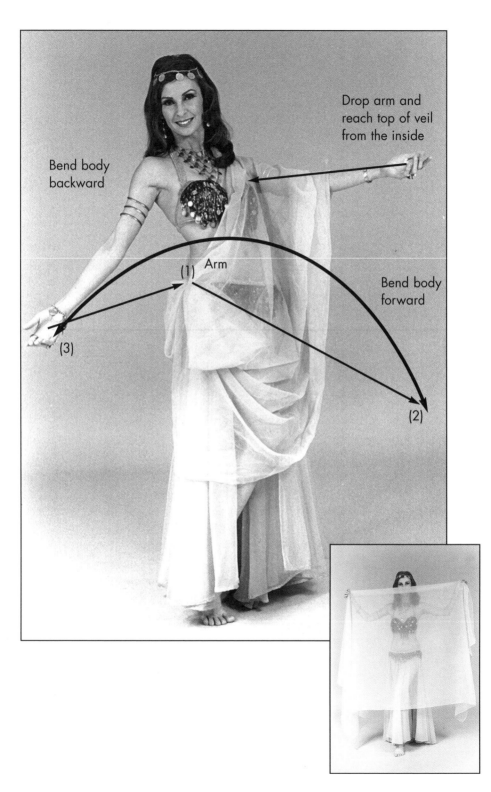

Drop arm and reach top of veil from the inside

Bend body backward

Bend body forward

(1) Arm

(2)

(3)

Veil - Removal

❖ At the end of a fast segment of music a drum roll will sound, spin around two or three times, and bow

❖ Do figure eight's and belly rolls. To remove the veil, drop the arm holding the veil, let the veil fall over the arm. Reach up on the inside of the veil and and grab the top edge

❖ Using the other arm, start pulling the tucked end from out of your belt (1)

❖ Bend your body over to the front, pulling your arm up and over to the front (2)

❖ Then bend to the back while pulling your arm up and backward (wax-on, wax-off)

❖ Start pulling the other side out in the same motion

❖ Soon you should have the veil pulled out on both sides

❖ Hold it in front of your face

Veil – Front Hold

❖ While holding the veil in front of your face

  ✦ Do head movements, figure 8's, two leg shimmy's, belly rolls

❖ Bring arms up together, wrapping the face with the veil

  ✦ Do belly rolls, head movements, two leg shimmy's, etc.

Veil – Side Wrap

❖ Take one arm and move it behind your back

❖ Take the other arm and raise it above your head and behind your head

  ✢ Do one leg shimmy's, and belly rolls

❖ Take a step, at the same time change arms to the other side

Veil – Body Circle

❖ Start in parallel position, with veil held in front

❖ Hold the veil stretched out in front of you and bend at the waist, way down in front

❖ Roll your body to the side, while moving your arms up and around your body

❖ Keep the roll going to the back. Your veil should be behind you

❖ Keep the roll going to the other side and back down in front.

❖ Be sure to bend as far to the front, side, back, side, and back down in front as possible

Keep the move slow.
Over exaggeration of this move
makes it much more exotic

Veil –
Roll Up and Toss

- ❖ Holding your veil in front of you, keep moving with two leg shimmy's, figure 8's, etc

- ❖ Slowly start rolling your veil up in your hands until you have it all rolled up

- ❖ Lift it up over your head. Head movements can be done here

- ❖ Continue moving it over your back to the back of your waist

- ❖ Switch your hands so you can hold the veil

- ❖ Stand in basic position and while rocking from front leg to back leg, start alternating your arms to make each side swing in circles at alternating times

- ❖ Stop while on the back leg, do one leg shimmy's, reach back with both hands, take the veil in one arm, and toss it out of your dancing way

Floor Work

Most of the time done to slow (or slower) music

Caution:
Do not do more than your body permits

Remember:
Do not go any further than your body permits.

Floor - Drop

◈ At the end of a fast segment of music a drum roll will sound, spin around two or three times

◈ Drop to your knees and lie back all the way to the ground

    ⚶ You can use your arm (hidden behind your back) to help lower yourself back to the ground

◈ While lying on the ground, do belly rolls

◈ If you cannot go all the back, just go down to your knees and sit between them

You can remove your cymbals if you wish and put them to the side of you.

Floor - Sitting Position

❖ Rise up from the lying down position while holding your arms in front of you *(if needed, you can use your elbow tucked behind your back as a help)*

❖ Come up to the sitting position

❖ Reach your arms on each side behind you on the floor

❖ Lift your hips up while supporting yourself on your arms

❖ Do hip thrust's, and belly rolls

Floor - Sway

❖ Sit on your knees

    ⚸ In this position you can do head movements, snake arms, shoulder rolls and bust shakes

❖ Rise up onto your knees and lean your hip way out to the side and pause

❖ Lower down to the middle and rise up on the other side (in a single movement), pause again

❖ Repeat

❖ Also up on the knees you can do head movements, shoulder rolls and bust shakes, belly rolls, and other arm movements

Floor Work - Half Wedge

(also called half Cleopatra)

❖ While sitting on your knees, take one arm and place it on the floor to the side of you. Slowly extend your top leg out. Now rise up onto the bent leg and support your lower body with your knee, support your upper body with your arm. The extended leg is there for balance. In this position do belly rolls and figure 8's. The upper leg can do one-leg shimmies

❖ Lower your hips back down to the floor

Floor Work - Full Wedge

(also called full Cleopatra)

(not for those physically challenged)

❖ While in half wedge and lowered to the floor, extend the other leg outward. Rise up onto your arm and balance on the balls of your feet. Do belly rolls in this position

❖ Lower your hips back down to the floor

❖ Return to sitting on your knees

Floor Work - Return to Standing

❖ While sitting on your knees, extend one leg outward

❖ Foot on the ground and knee bent, slowly rise up to standing position

Salute

At the end of the song, you will wish to thank your audience

***"From my heart, my words,
and my mind, I thank you"***

❖ Put your arm over your heart and bow
"From my heart. . ."

❖ Stand and put your hand over your lips
"my words. . ."

❖ Put your hand to your forehead
"and my mind. . . "

❖ Then take your hand out across your
audience (If you have a live band continue
your hand back to include the band)
"I thank you"

Summary

Remember:

Never Stop Moving

- ❖ While doing one move, think about the next move your are going to do

- ❖ Smooth transitions

- ❖ Take a step to go into the next move

- ❖ Count the transition step as a time beat

- ❖ When doing veil, always use shimmy's, figure 8's, or belly rolls while transitioning from one veil position to another

- ❖ Practice your zills at least 5 minutes every time you practice. And practice each move with your zills

*These are only some of the basic moves.
To become a good belly dancer you will
learn 100's of moves.*

*Find a good teacher, practice hard,
and you will become what you
wish to become!
Webas!*